AF316765

JONATHAN SWIFT (1667-1745) was born in Dublin, a posthumous son of English emigrants. When a year old, he was kidnapped to England by his nurse who restored him to his mother in Dublin, three years later. A poor relation and dependent, he was sent to grammar school and then to the Trinity College, Dublin, at the expense of his uncles. Swift received his BA degree from Trinity speciali gratia, *but his intentions to complete the requirements towards a Master's degree, too, were thwarted by the political turmoil that had the closing of the Trinity College as one of its results. It was some time later, while in England, that he finally got his Master's from Oxford, after he had been a secretary in the service of Sir William Temple, a retired diplomatist and protector of the Swift family. Jonathan Swift's subsequent Doctorate in Divinity was an honorary degree conferred on him by Trinity while he was Dean of St. Patrick in Dublin. Swift invested most of his wits and energy in pursuit of bettering himself, as he had been born without an inheritance. The best he could get was neither a position at Court nor even in England, but the deanery of St. Patrick's Cathedral in Dublin, with the Church of Ireland. Swift excelled as a political writer, and is best remembered for his dystopia known for short as GULLIVER'S TRAVELS. It seems rather characteristic of him to have bequeathed most of his fortune for the building and the endowment of a lunatic asylum in Dublin and the erection of public lavatories at Draper's Hill.*

PLUTARCH PRESS of Washington, D.C., is committed to the publication of works by or about classics of human thought from all over the world, that are relevant to our times, but which for no apparent reason are not in the limelight.

SERVICE IS NO INHERITANCE OR RULES TO SERVANTS according to the Rev. Dr.

J. Swift

To be read constantly
one night every week
upon going to bed

PLUTARCH PRESS
washington dc

This adaptation first published in the United States
by Plutarch Press, Washington, DC, 1987.

For information, address the publisher:
PLUTARCH PRESS
P.O. Box 39012, Washington, D.C. 20016-0412

Library of Congress Cataloging-in-Publication Data:

Draghici, Simona, 1937-
Service is no inheritance, or, Rules to servants according to the Rev. Dr. Swift.

Adaptation of: Directions to servants, 1745 / by Jonathan Swift.
1. Swift, Jonathan, 1667-1745. Directions to servants.
2. Domestics--Anecdotes, facetiae, satire, etc.
I. Swift, Jonathan, 1667-1745. Directions to servants, 1745. II. Title. III. Title: Rules to servants.
PR3724.D53S4 1987 824'.5 87-15113
ISBN 0-943045-01-0 (pbk.)

Manufactured in the United States of America.
Book design and vignettes by JAY.
Printed by BookCrafters Inc.,
Chelsea, Michigan.

EDITOR'S NOTE

In his Preface to A TALE OF A TUB, Jonathan Swift made a clean breast of his editorial difficulties in placing what was to be Section X of that book in the right position: 'I have chosen for it as proper a place as I could readily find. If the judicious reader can assign a fitter, I do here empower him to remove it to any other corner he pleases.' On my part, I have seized upon this very limited power of attorney in editorial matters bestowed on any judicious reader of the TALE, invoked it as a precedent and then extended it freely to another work of his, which he never managed to complete but which was published all the same soon after his death, as DIRECTIONS TO SERVANTS. In other words, the present adaptation of the 1745 London edition of that unfinished manuscript is meant to diminish the feeling of fragmentation experienced by any reader of the original. To that end, paragraphs have been reordered and repetitions and obscure details have been passed over. Likewise, the chapters that were barely sketched by their author have been omitted altogether. Here and there, words and phrases have been modernized. I am convinced that by this procedure the humour in which this little book is soaked would not turn stale or sour. In the process, I also decided to give it another, more general, title. On the one hand, it warns the pedant that this is not the scholarly edition that records all the variants of the Dean's text, which he might expect from the Oxford University Press, for instance. On the other hand, the new title, which by the way comes from Swift's book, underlines the issue which bothered Swift enough to make it the keystone of this particular work. Of this issue, which remains unresolved, I shall say more in the Commentary at the end of the book. In rest, I took the power of attorney granted by Swift too literally to insert any apocryphal additions of my own to his text, in order 'to make it look round and plump.'

It is also in the Commentary that I fully motivate my sociological interest in this posthumous work of Jonathan Swift's and show its relevance to us a quarter of a millenium after its conception.

Finally, the present book is dedicated to the memory of Ivy Compton-Burnett who turned Swift's topic into a novel.

S.D.

CONTENTS

GENERAL RULES CONCERNING ALL SERVANTS

When your master or lady call a servant by name and if that servant is not around, none of you is to answer. Otherwise, there will be no end of your drudgery. Even masters concede that a servant should come only when called. However do not come unless you have been called three or four times, for only a dog will come at the first whistle. When the master calls 'Someone there!!' no servant is bound to come. For 'Someone there' is nobody's name. If your master calls you by name and you happen to answer at the fourth call, you need not hurry yourself. And if you are scolded for taking so long to come, you may lawfully say that you came no sooner because you did not know what you were called for.

Never consent to stir a finger in any business but that for which you have been hired in effect. For example, if the groom is drunk or absent and the butler is ordered to shut the stable door, the latter should readily answer: 'Please Your Honour, I do not understand horses.' If a single nail is needed to fasten the corner of a hanging and the footman is told to tack it up, he may say that he knows nothing of that sort of work, but that His Honour may send for the upholsterer.

When you have done something wrong, be always pert and insolent, and behave as if you were the injured person. This will immediately put your master or lady off their mettle. As you go out of the room and down the stairs, mutter loud enough to be plainly heard. That will make your master believe that you are innocent.

When you are rebuked before company, which with all due respect to masters and ladies one must admit to be an unmannerly practice, one of the guests may happen to be good-natured enough to drop a word of excuse on your behalf. In this way you are given a generally acknowledged instrument by which to justify yourself. From it you may rightly conclude that whenever your master chides you afterwards, he may be wrong. You will be the better confirmed in your opinion by stating the case to your fellow-servants in your way. They will no doubt decide in your favour. Therefore, as I said before, whenever you are rebuked, complain as if you were the injured party.

If once in their lives, your master or lady happen to accuse you wrongfully, you are a lucky servant. All you have to do afterwards is to remind them of that false accusation every time you commit a fault while in their service, and to protest yourself equally innocent on each occasion thereafter.

There is nothing so pernicious in a household as a tell-tale. It must become the main business of you all to unite against him. Whatever office he serves in, take all the opportunities to upset the business he is about, and to cross him in everything. Thus, for instance, if the butler is the tell-tale, break his glasses whenever he leaves the pantry open, or lock the cat or the mastiff in it. They will do as well. Mislay a fork or a spoon, so that he may never find it. If it is the cook, whenever she turns her back, throw cinders and ashes or a handful of salt into the pot, or smoking coals into the dripping pan, or daub the roast with soot from the chimney, or hide the key of the jack. If the footman is suspected, let the cook daub the back of his new livery. Or when he is going up with a dish of soup, let her follow him quietly with a ladleful and drible it all the way up the stairs to the dining room, and then let the house-maid make such noise that her lady could hear it. The waiting-maid is very likely to be guilty of such a deed, keen as she is to ingratiate herself. In that case, the laundress must make sure to tear her smocks in the washing and then wash them by half only. When she complains, make the laundress tell all the house that she sweats so much and her skin is so nasty that in an hour's time she fouls a smock worse than the kitchen-maid does in a week.

If possible, never tell a lie to your master or lady, unless you have some hope that they cannot find out in less than half an hour. When a servant is turned off, all his faults must be revealed, although most of them were never known to his master or lady. All the mischiefs done by others should be charged to him. And if they ask why you never brought any of them to their attention, the answer should be: 'Sir (or Madam), really I was afraid it would make you angry. And besides, perhaps you might have thought it was malice in me.'

Where there are little masters and misses in the house, they usually are great impediments to the servants' diversions. The only remedy is to bribe them with goodie-goodies, that they may not tell tales to Papa and Mamma.

I do most earnestly exhort you all to unanimity and concord. But mistake me not: you may quarrel with each other as much as you please, only bear in mind that you have a common enemy, namely your master and lady, and that you have a common cause to defend. Believe an old practitioner: whoever out of malice to a fellow-servant carries a tale to his master shall be ruined by a general coalition against him.

The cook, the butler, the groom, the market-man and every other servant who is involved in the household expenses, should act as if his master's whole estate ought to be applied to that servant's particular business. Thus, for instance, if the cook computes the master's estate to amount to a thousand pounds a year, he or she would reasonably conclude that a thousand pounds a year will afford enough meat, and so need not be saving. The butler in turn makes the same judgment, and so may the groom and the coachman. Every branch of expense will be filled to to your master's honour.

If you are sent with ready money to buy anything at a shop and if at the time you happen to be short of cash yourself, sink the money and take up the goods on your master's account. It is for the honour of your master and of yourself. For he becomes a man of credit at your own recommendation.

Always take the tradesman's part against your master,

and when you are sent to buy anything, never offer to cheapen it. Rather pay generously in full what is demanded. This will bring honour to your master and, maybe, some shillings to your pocket. If your master has paid too much, he can better afford the loss than the poor tradesman.

It often happens that the servants sent on errands are apt to stay out longer than the delivery of the message requires. Perhaps two, four, six or even eight hours, or some such trifle. The temptation to be sure is great and blood and flesh cannot always resist. When you return, the master storms, the lady scolds. Stripping, cudgelling and turning off are the words they use. But on such occasions you ought to be provided with a set of excuses enough to serve you in all circumstances. Thus, for instance, your uncle came eighty miles to town in the morning, on purpose to see you, and goes back at the break of day, tomorrow. A brother servant who had borrowed money from you when he had been out of service, was running away to Ireland. You were taking leave of an old fellow-servant who was embarking for Barbados. Your father sent a cow for you to sell and you could not find a broker till nine at night. You were taking leave of a dear cousin who is to be hanged next Saturday. You wrenched your ankle against a stone and were forced to stay three hours in a shop before you could set down your foot again. Some nastiness was thrown on you out of a garret-window, and you were ashamed to come home before you were cleaned and the smell gone. You were pressed for service at sea and carried before a Justice of Peace who kept you three hours before he found time to examine you, and then you got off with much ado. A bailiff seized you by mistake for a debtor and kept you the whole evening in a sponging-house. You were told that your master had gone to a tavern and had some unfortunate accident, and your grief was so great that you inquired after His Honour in a hundred taverns between Pall Mall and Temple Bar.

When you stop to chat with some crony servant in the same street, leave your front door open that you may get in without knocking, when you come back. Otherwise, your lady may found out that you have been gone and scold you for it.

Whenever a servant comes home drunk and cannot appear before his master or lady, you must all join in telling your master that he has gone to bed very sick. On hearing that, your lady may be so good-natured and order some comfortable thing for the poor man or maid.

When your master or lady come home and want a servant who happens to be out, your answer must be that he has just stepped out, that very minute, being sent for by a cousin who is dying.

Whoever comes to visit your master or lady when they are out, never burden your memory with the visitor's name, for indeed you have so many other things to remember. Besides, it is a porter's business, and it is your master's fault that he does not keep one. And then who can remember names, anyway! You, for one, will certainly mistake them, as you can neither read nor write.

I advise the servants whose master lives in the country that whenever you expect tips from his guests, you should always stand rank and file when the stranger is taking his leave, so he could not help passing between you. If any of you let him escape, he must have more confidence than usual or less money. When he calls next time, remember to treat him according to his behaviour on this very last occasion.

Whenever your lady sends for you up to her chamber to give you orders, be sure to stand at the door and keep it open, fiddling with the lock all the while as she is talking to you. Keep the hand on the knob, for fear you would forget to close the door after you.

Masters and ladies are usually quarelling with their servants for not shutting the doors after them. Yet neither masters nor ladies take into account that the doors must be opened before they can be shut, and that the labour is double to open and then to shut each door. Therefore, the best, the shortest and the easiest way is to do neither. But if you are so often importuned to shut the door that you cannot easily forget it, then give the door such a bang when you go out, as will shake the whole room and make everything in it rattle. In that way, you make your master and lady be in no doubt that you heed their directions without demur.

On having noticed that the maids and fellows below stairs often forget to shut the door after them as they come and go out into the back yard, some nice ladies, who are afraid of catching cold, have ordered that a pulley and rope with a large piece of lead at the end should be so fixed as to make the door shut of itself. It requires a strong arm to open it, which is an immense toil to the servants whose business may force them to go in and out fifty times in any one morning. But ingenuity can do much, and so prudent servants have contrived an effective remedy against the insufferable grievance. They tie up the pulley in such a way that the weight of the lead will have no effect. However, if I were you, I would rather choose to keep the door always open by laying a heavy stone at its bottom.

Whenever your master and lady go out to dinner together, or on a visit for the evening, you need leave only one servant in the house, unless you have a menial boy to answer the door and attend the children, if there are any. Who is to stay behind will be decided by drawing lots. The servant left at home may be comforted by a visit from a a sweetheart, without the risk of being caught together. Such opportunities should never be missed because they are rare, and all is safe enough while there is a servant in the house.

The general meeting place for all servants, both in winter and in summer, is the kitchen. There, the grand affairs of the household ought to be discussed. Whether they concern the stable, the dairy, the pantry, the laundry, the cellar, the nursery, the dining-room, or my lady's chamber. There, as in your proper element, you can laugh and scream and romp in full security.

Let it be a constant rule that no chair, stool or table in the servants' hall, or in the kitchen, shall have more than three legs. That has been the ancient and constant custom in all the households I ever knew. It is said to be founded on two reasons: first, to show that servants are ever in a tottering conditions; second, it is thought to be a token of their humble condition that the servants' chairs and tables should have at least one leg less than those of their masters'. I grant however that there has been an exception to this rule, as far as the cook is concerned. By an old custom, she is allowed an easy chair to sleep in after dinner. Yet I have seldom seen any with more than three legs. Philosophers impute this epidemical lameness of servants' chairs to two causes which have been noticed to make the greatest revolutions in states and empires. By that I mean love and war. A stool, a chair or a table are the first weapons taken up in a general romping or skirmish. And after peace is restored, the chairs are apt, if not very strong, to suffer further in the conduct of a love-affair: the cook being usually fat and heavy and the butler a little in his cups.

Write your own name and that of your sweetheart with the smoke of a candle on the ceiling of the kitchen, or of the servants' hall, to show your learning.

Whatever good bits you can pilfer in the day-time, save them to junket with your fellow-servants at night, and take in the butler, provided he will give you the drink.

Whenever you invite the neighbouring servants to junket with you at home in the evening, teach them a particular way of tapping or scraping at the kitchen-window, so you may hear, but not your master or lady. You must take care not to disturb or frighten the latter at such unseasonable hours.

Although you are allowed knives for the servants' hall at meals, still you ought to spare them, and make use only of your master's.

As soon as you have broken all your earthen drinking vessels below the stairs, which is usually done in a week's time, the copper pot will do as well. It can boil milk, heat porridge, hold light beer, or in case of necessity, could be used as a jordan. Apply it indifferently to all these uses, but never wash or scour it, for fear of taking off the tin.

Whenever you want proper instruments for any work you are about, use all expedients you can invent, rather than leave the work undone. Thus, for instance, if the poker is out of reach or broken, stir up the fire with the tongs. If the tongs are not at hand, use the muzzle of the bellows, the wrong end of the fire shovel, the handle of the fire brush, the end of a mop, or your master's cane. If you want to singe a fowl, tear the first book you see about the house. Wipe your shoes with the bottom of any curtain, for want of a cloth, or with a damask napkin. Likewise, I could never bear to see maid servants so ungenteel as to walk the streets with their pettycoats pinned up. It is a foolish excuse to allege that their pettycoats will be dirty when they have such an easy remedy in walking three or four times down a clean pair of stairs after they come home. Strip your livery lace for garters and if the butler is in dire need of a jordan, he may use the great silver bowl.

The servants' candlesticks are generally broken, for nothing can last for ever. But you may easily find many other substitutes. You may conveniently stick your candle in a bottle. Or, by means of a lump of butter, you may stick it against the wainscot. You may stick it in a powder horn, an old shoe, or in a cleft stick, in the barrel of a pistol, or upon its own grease on a table. You may also consider a coffee cup, or a drinking glass, a horn can, or a teapot, a twisted napkin, a mustard pot, an ink horn, a marrowbone, a piece of dough, or you may cut a hole in a loaf and stick the candle there.

There are several ways of putting out candles and you ought to be instructed in all of them. You may run the candle end against the wainscot, which puts the snuff out immediately. You may lay it on the floor and tread the snuff out with your feet. You may hold it upside down until it is choked with its own grease, or cram it upside down into the socket of the candlestick. You may whirl it round until it goes out. The cook may run the nose of the candle into the meal tub, or the groom may sink it into a bucket of oats, or run it against a tuft of hay, or a heap of litter. The house-maid may put out her candle by running it against a looking-glass, as nothing cleans it so well as candle snuff. When you go to bed, after you passed water, you may dip the candle end into the chamber pot. You also may choose to spit on your forefinger and thumb, and then pinch the snuff until it goes out. But the quickest and best of all methods is to blow it out with your breath, which leaves the candle clear and readier to be lighted again.

If you are a young and rather good-looking fellow attending at the table, run your nose fully in your lady's cheek whenever you have to whisper something in her ear. Or, if your breath is good, breathe fully in her face. This I know to have had very good consequences in some families.

If you find yourself growing in favour with your master or lady, take some occasion, in a very mild way, to give them warning. When they ask the reason and seem loathe to part with you, answer that you would rather stay with them than with anybody else, but a poor servant is not to be blamed if he strives to better himself. Tell them that service is no inheritance, that your work is more than what it ought to be and your wages are very small. Then, if your master has any generosity, he will add five to ten shillings a quarter, rather then let you go. But if you are disappointed in your move and have no mind to leave, then get some fellow-servant to tell your master that he has prevailed upon you to stay.

When you have really made up your mind to leave your master, but are too shy to break the news to him for fear of angering him, your best way is to grow rude and insolent all of a sudden, beyond your usual behaviour, until he finds it necessary to turn you off. Then, in revenge, when you are gone, give such a character of him and of his lady to all your brother servants on the look for a place, that none will venture to offer their services.

And whatever you do, remember to lay all the faults on a lap dog, a favourite cat, a monkey, a parrot, a child, or on the servant who was last dismissed from service. By this rule, you will excuse yourself, do no harm to anybody else, and spare your master or lady the trouble and vexation of scolding.

THE BUTLER

I find from my long experience that you, butler, are the principal party concerned in my directions to servants.

Your business is of great variety and requires the greatest precision. So to my best of abilities, I shall run through the several branches of your office, and arrange my instructions accordingly.

When you dress up your sideboard, set the best glasses as near the edge of the table as you can. In this way, they will cast a double lustre and make a much finer figure. The consequences can be at worst but the breaking of half a dozen of them, which is a trifle to your master's pocket.

Because butlers often forget to bring up their ale and beer in good time, be sure to remember to have yours up two hours before dinner. Place them in the sunny part of the room to let people see that you have not been negligent.

In waiting at the sideboard, take all possible care to save your own trouble and your master's drink and glasses. Thus, remember that since those who dine at the same table are supposed to be friends, let them all drink from the same glass without washing.Give no person liquor unless he has called at least three times for it. In that way, some out of modesty and others out of forgetfulness will call less often and so your master's liquor will be saved.

If anyone desires a glass of bottled ale, first shake the bottle to see whether anything is in it, then taste it, to find out what kind of liquor it is, and so you will avoid a mistake, and lastly, wipe the mouth of the bottle with the palm of your hand to show your cleanliness.

There is an excellent method devised in recent years about how to handle ale and light beer at the sideboard.Let us say, for instance, that a gentleman calls for a glass of ale and then drinks but half of it, and another calls for light beer. You immediately pick up the half-empty glass of ale and pour out the remainder in the tankard, and then fill the glass with light beer; and so backwards and forwards as long as your dinner lasts. By doing just that you attain three great ends: one, you save yourself the trouble of washing the glasses, and consequently you are in no danger of breaking them; two, you are sure to make no mistake in giving the gentlemen the drinks they call for, and three, by using this method you are certain that nothing is wasted.

If one calls for light beer towards the end of the meal, do not give yourself the pains of going down to the cellar, but drain into one cup all that has been left in the other cups, glasses and salvers. While you are doing that, make sure to turn your back to the company, for fear of being observed. On the contrary, if anyone calls for ale towards the end of the dinner, fill the largest tankard to the brim. In this way you will have most of it left to oblige your fellow-servants below stairs without the sin of stealing from your master.

Another honest perquisite is that of getting the best part of a bottle of wine for yourself every day. You are not to suppose that gentlefolks will value the remainder of a bottle, once it has been uncorked and served from. Therefore, always set a fresh bottle before them after dinner, even though no more than a glassful has been poured out of the other.

Be more careful to have the cork in the belly of the bottle than in the mouth. And if the cork is musty or some white filaments are floating in the liquor, your master will save the more.

A good butler always breaks off the point of the corkscrew in two days by trying which is harder: the point of the screw or the neck of the bottle. In such a case, when the screw turns to be of little use after the stump has torn the cork into pieces, fetch instead a silver fork and when the scraps of cork are almost drawn, shake the neck of the bottle briskly into the cistern, three or four times, until you quite clear it.

Some butlers have a way of decanting bottled ale that they waste a good part of the bottom. Let your method be the following: turn the bottle directly upside down, which will make the liquor appear double the quantity. By this means you will be sure not to waste a drop, and besides, the froth will conceal the muddiness.

Put your finger into every bottle to feel whether it is full; that is the surest way: for feeling has no match.

You need not wipe your knife to cut bread for the table, because in cutting a slice or two it will wipe itself.

Whet the backs of the knife blades until they are as sharp as the edges. That will be an advantage: when the gentlemen find them blunt on one side, they may try the other. Moreover, to show that you spare no pains in the sharpening of knives, whet them so long that a good part of the blade and even the silver handle are worn out. That does credit to your master, for it shows good housekeeping. And one day, the silversmith may make you a present.

That the salt may lie smooth in the salt-cellar, press it down with your moist palm.

When the salt is spilled on the table, do not let it be wasted. As soon as dinner is over, fold up the tablecloth with the salt in it, then shake the salt out into the salt-cellar to serve next day. But the shortest and surest way, when removing the cloth, is to wrap the knives, forks, spoons, salt-cellars, broken bread and scraps of meat all together into the tablecloth. By which you will be sure to lose nothing, unless you think it better to shake them out of the window amid the beggars, so they may eat the scraps with more convenience.

If a gentleman forgets his snuff-box or toothpick case on the table after dinner and departs without remembering it, look upon it as part of your tips. For so it is admitted by all servants and moreover, you do no wrong to your master or lady.

After supper, if it is dark, carry your plate and china together in the same basket, to save candle-light. You know your pantry well enough to put them back in the dark.

Always lock up a cat in the closet where you keep the china plates, for fear the mice may steal in and break them.

Clean your plate, wipe your knives and rub the dirty table with the napkins and the tablecloth used that day. For it is but one washing. Besides, you save wearing out the coarse rubbers. As a reward for such good husbandry you may lawfully get the finest damask napkins made into nightcaps for yourself.

When you clean your plate, leave the polish to be seen in all the chinks, for fear your lady should believe you had not cleaned it.

Leave the dregs of ale, wine and other liquors in the bottles. To rinse them is but loss of time, since all this will be done eventually in a general washing. Besides, you will have a better excuse for breaking them.

If your master has many musty or very dirty and crusted bottles, I sincerely advise you to trade them before any other for ale or brandy at the nearest ale-house.

When you are to get hot water on, for tea after dinner, which in many households is part of your office, to save fuel and to make more haste, pour it into the tea-kettle from the pot where cabbage or fish have been boiling. That will make it much more wholesome by curing the acid quality of the tea.

When you cut bread for toast, do not stand idly watching it, but lay it on the coals and mind your other business. Then come back, and if you find it toasted quite through, scrape off the burned side and serve it up.

When a gentleman is leaving after he has dined with your master, be sure to stand in his full sight and follow him to the door and look him square in the face, if you have a chance, because it may bring you a shilling. But if the gentleman has spent the night in your master's house then get the cook, the house-maid, the stable-man, the scullion and the gardener to accompany you. You should stand all in his way to the entrance hall, in a line on each side of him. If the gentleman performs handsomely, it will do him honour and cost your master nothing. However, if a gentleman dines often with your master and gives you nothing when he goes away, you may use several methods to show him some token of your displeasure and quicken his memory. Thus, if he calls for bread or drink, you may pretend not to hear, or send them to another who called after him. If he asks for wine, let him wait awhile, and then send him light beer. Give him always dirty glasses. Send him a spoon when he wants a knife. Wink at the footman to leave him without a plate. By these expedients and the like, you may perhaps be a better man by half a crown before he leaves the house, provided you watch for the opportunity of standing by when he takes his leave.

At times, a humble guest, a chaplain, a tutor, or a dependent cousin may happen to be at table and you are likely to find that your master and the company have little regard for that person. Nobody is readier to notice that than the servants. In such circumstances, you and the footman must follow the example of your betters and treat him as many degrees worse than any of the rest. You cannot please your master better, or at least your lady.

If you serve a country squire, and ladies and gentlemen come to dine at your master's house, never fail to make their servants drunk, and especially the coachmen. That will be to the honour of your master. In all your actions you must have a special regard for it, since you are its best judge: the honour of any household lies in the hands of the butler, the cook and the groom as I will demonstrate. Likewise, whenever a message is brought to your master, be kind to your brother servant who carries it. Give him the best liquor in your keeping, for your master's honour. And with the first occasion he will do the same to you.

When company is expected at dinner or in the evening, be sure to take off and also that nothing may be got which is under your key. In that way your master will save his liquor, as well as his plate.

If you are curious to taste some of your master's choice bottles, empty as many of them just below the neck as will make the amount you want. But then take care to fill them up again with clean water, that you may not lessen your master's liquor.

I come now to a most important part of your economy: the bottling of a hogshead of wine. For that I recommend three virtues: cleanliness, frugality and brotherly love.

Take special care that your bottles are not musty, before you fill them. Blow strongly into the mouth of every bottle and then, if you smell nothing but your own breath, fill them immediately. As to your bottles,choose the smallest you can find, which will increase the number of dozens and so please your master. A bottle of wine is always a bottle of wine, whether it can hold more or less. If your master has his proper number of dozens, he cannot complain. But first, they must be rinsed with wine, for fear of any moisture left from the washing. Some, out of misplaced thrift, will rinse a dozen bottles with the same wine. But I would advise you to be more cautious and change the wine at every second bottle. A quarter-pint may be enough. Have bottles ready to empty into. It will be a good perquisite either to sell or to drink with the cook.

You may also consider to wash your bottles immediately before you begin, but make sure not to drain them, and by such good management your master will save some gallons in every hogshead. If your master finds the hogshead to fall short of his expectations, what is plainer than that the cask leaked! That the wine-cooper had not filled it in the proper time! That the merchant cheated by sending a hogshead below the common measure!

Let your corks be the longest kind you can find. That will save some wine in the neck of every bottle. Fill your mouth full of corks together with a large plug of tobacco which will give the wine the true taste of the weed, so delightful to all good judges of wine.

Never draw your hogshead too low. Nor tilt it, for fear

of disturbing the liquor. When it begins to run slow and before the wine grows cloudy, shake the hogshead and carry a glass of it to your master who will praise your discretion and give you all the rest as a privilege of your place in the household. You may tilt the hogshead next day and in a fortnight get a dozen or two of good clear wine out of it to dispose of as you please.

This is the occasion that in honour of your master you ought to show your kindness to your fellow-servants, and especially to the cook. What do a few flasks out of a whole hogshead count for! But make them be emptied in your presence, for fear that they would be given to other people, and so your master would be wronged. But advise them that if they get drunk to go to bed without delay and leave word that they are sick. I would have all the servants, both male and female, be that cautious.

When you are ordered to decant a suspect bottle, as soon as a pint is out, give your hand a defty shake and show it in a glass that it is turning muddy.

When you go down to the cellar to draw ale or light beer, take care to follow closely the method I am describing now: hold the vessel between the forefinger and the thumb of your right hand with the palm upwards. Then hold the candle between the other fingers, yet leaning a little towards the mouth of the vessel. Take out the spigot with your left hand and stick its pointed end into your mouth. All the while keep your left hand to watch for accidents. When the vessel is full, take the spigot out of your mouth, well wetted with spittle which being slimy will make it stick faster into the faucet. If any tallow drops into the vessel, you may easily remove it, if need be, with a spoon or rather with your finger.

If you are sent down in haste to draw any drink and find it will not run, do not bother to open the vent. Blow strongly into the faucet and you will find the liquor pour immediately into your mouth. Or you may remove the peg, but do not stay to stop the vent again,for fear your master should want you.

Nowhere does the skill of a butler show more than in the management of candles. Although some part may fall to the share of other servants, you are the main person concerned. In consequence, I shall direct my instructions upon this item to you alone, leaving your fellow-servants to apply them on occasion.

Firstly, to avoid burning them in daylight and to save your master's candles, never bring them up until half an hour after dark, although they may be called for, ever so often.

Let the sockets fill with grease to the brim, with the old snuff at the top, then stick on your fresh candles. It is true that in this way they are in danger of falling, but the candles will appear so much longer and handsomer to your master's guests. At other times, for a change, put your candles loose in the sockets to show that they have been cleaned to the bottom.

When a candle is too big for the socket, melt it to the right size in the fire, and to hide the smut, wrap the candle in paper half way up.

One cannot help noticing the great extravagance among the gentry with regard to the article of candles these last years. A good butler ought by all means to discourage it, in order to spare both himself and his master's money. This may be attained in several ways. Let us say that you are ordered to put candles in the sconces, for instance. Now, sconces are great wasters of candles, and you, who are always to hold your master's interests at heart, should do your utmost to discourage their use. Therefore you are to press the candle with both your hands into the socket and make it lean in such a way as the grease may drop all on the floor, unless some lady's head-dress or gentleman's periwig are not at hand to intercept it. Likewise, you may stick the candle so loose that it will fall upon the glass of the sconce and break it suddenly to shatters. In this way you will save your master many a fair penny in candles in the course of a year. To the glazier and yourself it will save much toil, for once damaged, the sconces cannot be used again.

Or you may consider an alternative. Be saving of your candles, and let those in the hall and on the stairs, in the sconces and in the lantern, burn down into the sockets until they go out by themselves. As soon as they will smell the snuff, your master and lady will commend your thrift.

Still another method to save is never to let the candles burn too low, but give what is left of them to the cook, your friend, to add to her kitchen supplies. Or, if that is not allowed in your household, give them to the poor neighbours in charity, for they often run on your errands.

Snuff the candles at supper as they stand on the table. That is by far the safest way, because if the burning snuff happens to get out of the snuffers, there is a chance that it may fall into a dish of soup, posset, rice-milk or the like, where it will be immediately extinguished with very little stink.

Whenever you have snuffed the candles, always leave the snuffers open; in that way the snuff will burn of itself away to ashes and cannot fall out and dirty the table when you snuff the candles again.

If your lady loves to play cards, your fortune is made for ever. Moderate gambling will bring you ten shillings a week in revenue. In such a household I would rather be the butler than the chaplain or even the steward. It is all ready cash and got without labour, unless your lady happens to be one of those who insist on wax candles or forces you to share your earnings with her favourite servants. At worst, the old cards are yours. Whenever the gamblers play secretively or grow irritable, they will change cards as so often. The old packs will get you a considerable profit by selling them to coffee-houses or to households that love playing but cannot afford better cards than second-hand. Whenever you are in attendance at such parties, be sure to leave new packs within the reach of the guests, for those who have ill luck will readily take them, in the hope that they will change their fortune. And now and then, an old pack mingled with the rest will easily pass. Remember to be very efficient on play-nights, and ready with candles to light out the company of guests. Have salvers of wine at hand to give them when they call, but come to an understanding with the cook that no supper will be provided. It will represent such a saving to the household. On the other hand, serving supper will considerably reduce your gains.

Next to cards, there is nothing so profitable to you as bottles, and in this area you have no competitors, save the footmen who are apt to steal and sell them for pots of beer. But you are bound to prevent such abuses in your master's household. The footmen are not to answer for what is broken at a general bottling. On such occasions, as many bottles may break as your discretion will make them.

The profit from glasses is so inconsiderable that it is hardly worth mentioning. It consists only in the small presents made to you by the glassman, and about four shillings in the pound added to their price for the trouble you take and your skill in choosing them. If your master has a large stock of them and you or your fellow-servants happen to break any of the glasses without your master becoming aware of it, keep it secret until not enough of them are left to serve the table. Then tell your master that there are no more glasses. This will be but one annoyance to him, which is so much better than making him fret once or twice a week. It is the duty of a good servant to upset his master and lady as seldom as he can. And here the cat and the dog will be of great use to take the blame from you.

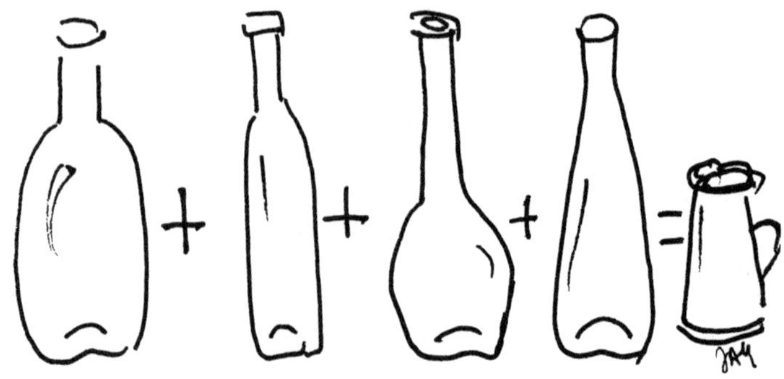

THE COOK

I am not ignorant of the fact that it has long now been a custom among people of quality to keep men cooks, and generally of French nationality. Yet, because my treatise is chiefly calculated for the general run of knights, squires and gentlemen both in town and country, I shall therefore apply to you Mrs. Cook as a woman. However, a great part of what I intend to say may serve for either sex. Your position follows naturally that of the butler, because he and you are joined in interest. The tips of you both are generally equal and paid, too, while the others may be disappointed. You can feast together at night upon your own fare, when the rest of the house are abed. You also have it in your power to make every fellow-servant your friend. You can give a good bit or a little sup to the little masters and misses, and gain their affections. A quarrel between you and the butler is very dangerous for you both, and will probably end in one of you being dismissed from service. In so fatal a case, perhaps it will not be so easy for some time to cotton with another. And now, Mrs. Cook, I proceed to give you my instructions which I want you to get some fellow-servant in the household to read to you constantly one night every week upon your going to bed, whether you serve in town or in the country. My lessons will suit both.

If your lady forgets that there is any cold meat in the house, do not be so officious to remind her. It is plain that she does not want it. Therefore, dispose of it with the butler, or any other crony, before you go to bed. If she remembers it the next day, say that she gave you no orders, and besides, it was consumed, and so you need not tell her a lie.

Never send up a leg of a fowl at supper as long as there there is a cat or a dog in the house, that can be accused of running away with it. But if there happens to be neither, you must lay it upon the rats or a stray greyhound.

If your lady orders you to set up a piece of meat for supper, you are not to understand that you must set it up *all*. Therefore, you may give half to yourself and the butler.

If you live in a wealthy household, roasting and boiling are below the dignity of your office. It becomes you to be ignorant of them. Therefore, leave that work wholly to the kitchen wench, for fear of disgracing the household you live in.

Get three or four char-women constantly to attend you in the kitchen, whom you pay a low rate, that is to say, only with remains from meals, a few coals and all the cinders.

Good cooks cannot stand what they very justly call fiddling work, that is to say, when abundance of time is spent and little is done. Such is the dressing and stuffing of all little birds, which requires a world of cookery and fuss, as well as a second or a third spit. That, by the way, is absolutely needless. It would be a very ridiculous thing indeed, if a spit which is strong enough to turn a sirloin of beef should not be able to turn a lark. However, if your lady is nice and is afraid that a large spit will tear them, place them handsomely in the dripping pan, where the fat of roasted mutton or beef falling on the birds will serve to baste them. So you save both time and butter. For what cook of any spirit would waste time in picking larks, wheaters and other small birds! Therefore, if you cannot get the maids or the young misses to assist you, just make short work, and either singe or flay them. There is no great loss in the skins, and the flesh is just the same.

If your mistress allows you the kitchen-stuff, in return for her generosity, take care to boil and roast your meat sufficiently. If she keeps them for her own profit, do her justice: rather than let a good fire be wanting, enliven it now and then with the dripping and the butter that happens to turn to oil.

Send up your meat well stuck with skewers, to make it look round and plump. An iron skewer, rightly used now and then, will make it look handsomer. When you roast a long joint of meat, be careful only about the middle, and leave the two ends raw. They may serve another time, and in this way you will also save fuel.

Let a red-hot coal now and then fall into the dripping pan, that the smoke of the dripping may ascend and give the roast meat a high taste.

If a lump of soot falls into the soup and you cannot conveniently get it out of the pot, stir it in well. It will give the soup a high French taste.

When you send up butter for sauce, be so thrifty to let it be half water, which is also much more wholesome.

If you melt your butter to oil, do not worry, but send it up. For oil is a more refined sauce than butter.

If you are employed in shopping, buy your meat as cheap as you can. But when you bring in your accounts, be tender of your master's honour: set down the highest rate. Besides, it is but justice: for nobody can afford to sell at the same rate that one buys. I am confident that you may always safely swear that you gave no more than what the butcher and poulterer asked. On the other hand, when in the market, do not accept a treat of beefsteak and pot of ale from the butcher. In all conscience I think it to be no better than wronging your master. But do always take that gratuity in money, if you do not buy on credit, or as a commission per pound weight when you pay the bills.

Let a menial boy be always about the house to send on your errands and to go to market for you on rainy days. That will save your clothes and make you appear more creditable to your lady. However, if you find it necessary to go to market on a wet day, take your mistress' riding-hood and cloak to save your own clothes.

Always keep a large fire in the kitchen whenever there is a small dinner, or the family dines out. Seeing the smoke, the neighbours may commend your master's housekeeping. But whenever much company is invited, then be as sparing as possible of your coals. In that way, remaining half raw, a great deal of the meat will be saved, and will serve for the day after.

In roasting and boiling, order the kitchen-maid to bring none but the large coals, and save the small ones for the fires above the stairs. The former are more suitable for dressing the meat. Then, when they are out and furthermore if you happen to spoil any dish, you may fairly lay the blame upon the lack of coals. Besides, the cinder-pickers will be sure to speak ill of your master's housekeeping were they not to find plenty of large cinders mixed with fresh large coals. Thus you may dress your meat with credit, perform an act of charity, enhance the honour of your master and sometimes get a share of a pot of ale for your bounty towards the cinder-women.

When you have plenty of fowl in the larder, take pity of the poor cat, if she is a good mouser, and leave the door open.

Never clean your spits after they have been used. The grease left upon them by the meat is the best thing to protect them from rust. And when you make use of them again, the same grease will keep the inside of the meat moist.

Never make use of a spoon in any thing that you can do with your hands, for fear of wearing out your master's plate.

When you scour your plates and dishes, bend the brim inward in order to make them hold the more.

Scrape the bottoms of your pots and kettles with a silver spoon, for fear of giving them a taste of copper.

If your butter tastes of brass when it is melted, it is your master's fault for not allowing you a silver saucepan. It will save butter, and beside, new tinning is so very expensive. If you have a silver saucepan and the butter smells of smoke, lay the fault upon the coals.

If you have a silver saucepan for the kitchen use, let

me advise you to batter it well and keep it always black. Make room for the saucepan by wriggling it on the coals. This will be for your master's honour, because it shows that there has been constant good housekeeping. And in the same manner, if you are allowed a large silver spoon for the kitchen, have its bowl worn out with continuous scraping and stirring, and keep saying merrily: 'This spoon owes my master no service.'

If you send up a mess of broth, water-gruel or the like to your master in the morning, do not forget to put salt with your thumb and two fingers on the side of the plate. For if you make use of a spoon, or the end of a knife, there may be danger that the salt would fall, and that will be a sign of ill luck. Only remember to lick your thumb and fingers clean, before you offer to touch the salt.

As the kitchen bellows are usually out of order with stirring the fire with the muzzle to save tongs and poker, borrow the bellows from your lady's bed-chamber, which are commonly the best in the house, because they are the least used. And if you happen to damage or grease them, you have a chance to keep them entirely for your own use.

To keep troublesome servants out of the kitchen, always leave the winder sticking on the jack to fall on their heads.

You are to look upon your kitchen as your dressing-room. But you are not to wash your hands till you have gone to the necessary house, and spitted your meat, trussed your pullets, picked your sallad, nor indeed, until after you have sent up the second course. For your hands will become ten times dirty with the many things you are forced to handle. But when your work is over, one washing will serve for all.

There is but one aspect of your grooming that I would admit of, while the victuals are boiling, roasting or stewing. By that I mean the combing of your hair, which takes no time, because you can stand over your cooking and watch it with one hand, while you are using your comb with the other.

If some of your combings happen to be sent up with the victuals, you may safely lay the blame upon any of the footmen that has vexed you. Those gentlemen are sometimes apt to be malicious if you refuse them a sop in the pan, or a slice from the spit. They are even more so when you discharge a ladleful of hot porridge on their legs, or send them up to their masters with a dish-cloth pinned to their tails.

Let there always be a strict friendship between you and the butler, for it is in the interest of you both to be united. The butler often wants a comfortable tit-bit, and you much oftener a cool cup of good liquor. However, be on the look out when dealing with him, for sometimes he is not constant in his love. He has the great advantage of alluring the maids with a glass of sack, or white wine and sugar.

When you roast a breast of veal, remember that your sweetheart, the butler, loves a sweetbread. Therefore, set it aside until evening. You can say: 'The cat or the dog has run away with it;' or that you found it tainted or fly-blown. Besides, the roast looks as well on the table without the sweetbread as with it.

When you find that you cannot get dinner ready at the appointed time, put the clock back, and then it may be ready to the minute.

Whenever you are in haste to take down your dishes, tip them in such a manner that a dozen will fall together upon the dresser, just ready for your hand.

It is bad housekeeping to soil your kitchen rubbers by wiping the bottoms of the dishes you send up, since the table-cloth will do as well, and is changed every meal.

To save time and trouble, cut your apples and onions with the same knife, for well-bred gentry love the taste of an onion in everything they eat.

Lump three or four pounds of butter together with your

hands, then dash it against the wall just over the dresser, so as to have it ready to pull by pieces when you need it.

When you make the company wait long for dinner and the meat is overdone, you may lawfully lay the blame on your lady who so hurried you to send up dinner, that you were forced to send it up too much boiled and roasted.

If your dinner fails in almost every dish, how could you help it! You were teased by the footmen coming into the kitchen. And to prove it true, take the occasion to be angry and throw a ladleful of broth on one or two of their liveries. Moreover, Friday and Childermas-day are two cross days in the week, and that it is impossible to have good luck on either of them. Therefore, on those two days you have a lawful excuse.

As soon as you have sent up the second course, you have nothing to do in a great household until supper. Therefore, scour your hands and face, put on your bonnet and scarf and take your pleasure among your cronies till nine or ten at night....But dine first.

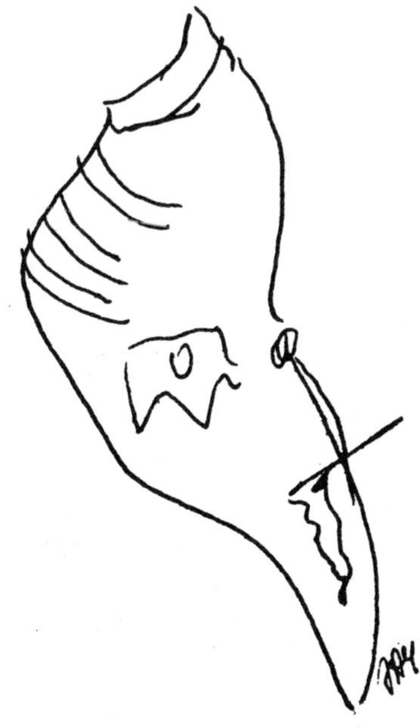

THE FOOTMAN

Being of a mixed nature, your employment extends to a great variety of tasks. You also stand in a fair way of being the favourite of your master or lady, or of the young masters or misses. You are the fine gentleman of the household, with whom all the maids are in love. Sometimes you are a pattern of dress to your master, and other times, he is to you. You wait at table in all companies and consequently have the opportunity to see and know the world and to understand men and manners. I must admit that your tips are but few, unless you are sent with a present, or to attend the tea in the country. But you are called Mr. in the neighbourhood, and sometimes pick up a fortune, perhaps your master's daughter. I have known many of your tribe to have good commissions in the Army. In town, you have a seat reserved for you in the playhouse, where you have an opportunity of becoming wits and critics. Learn all the new-fashion words and oaths, and songs and scraps of plays that your memory can hold. Thus you will become the delight of nine ladies in ten and the envy of ninety-nine beaux in a hundred. You have no professed enemy except the rabble and My Lady's waiting-maid. They are sometimes apt to call you 'lackey.' I have a true veneration for your office, because I had once the honour of being one of your order which I foolishly left by demeaning myself into accepting an employment with the custom-house. But in order that you, my brethern, may come to better fortunes, I shall here deliver my instructions. They are the fruit of much thought and observation, as well as of seven years' experience.

Never be seen in the street with a basket or a bundle in your hands. Carry nothing but what you can hide in your pocket. Otherwise you will disgrace your calling.To prevent that, always retain a menial boy to carry your loads. And if you are short of farthings, pay him with a good slice of bread or scrap of meat.

If you can, choose a service where your livery colours are least tawdry and eye-catching. Green and yellow immediately betray your office. So do all kinds of lace, except silver, which will hardly fall to your share, unless you come to serve with a duke, or some prodigal just come to his estate. The colours you ought to wish for are blue or dead leaf, turned up with red. That, together with a borrowed sword, a borrowed air, your master's linen, and a natural and improved confidence will give you what title you please, in whatever place your are not known.

If your master or lady happen to walk in town, keep on one side of the street, and as much on the level with them as you can. Noticing it, people will either think you do not belong to them, or that you are one of their companions. But if either of them happen to turn back and speak to you, in which case you need to take off your hat, use but your thumb and one finger, and scratch your head with the rest.

Always wear your hat in the house, but when your master calls. As soon as you come in his presence, pull it off to show your manners.

There is no indignity so great to one of your station, as that of lighting your master in the streets with a lantern. Therefore, it is very honest policy to try all arts to avoid it. Besides, it shows your master to be either poor or covetous, which are the two worst qualities you can meet with in any service. I made use of several wise expedients when I was in such a situation, and here I recommend them to you. Sometimes I took a candle so long that it reached to the very top of the lantern and burnt it. But after a good beating, my master ordered me to paste the top with paper. Then I used a middling candle, but stuck it so loose in the socket that it leaned towards one side and burnt a whole quarter of the horn. Then I used a bit of candle, less than half an inch, which sunk in the socket and melted the solder. It forced my master to walk half the way in the dark. Then he made me stick two inches of candle in the place where the socket was. After that I pretended to stumble, put out the candle, and broke the tin part to pieces. At last, he was forced to make use of a lantern-boy out of perfectly good husbandry.

Whenever you are ordered to call a coach, although it may be midnight, go no farther than the door, for fear of being out of reach when you are wanted. Stand there bawling: 'Coach, coach!' for half an hour.

If your lady sends you for a hackney-coach on a wet day, come back in the coach to save your clothes and also the trouble of walking. Better the hems of her petticoats be daggled with your dirty shoes than your livery spoiled and yourself getting a cold.

Never clean your shoes on the scraper, but in the entry, or at the foot of the stairs. In this way you will have the advantage of being at home a minute sooner, and the scraper will last longer.

When you attend your lady in a dark night, if she uses her coach, do not walk by the coach side so as to tire and dirty yourself. Rather get up and take your proper place in the seat behind and hold the flambeau sloping over the coach roof. Whenever it needs snuffing, dash it against the corners of the coach roof.

Whenever you are sent with a message, deliver it in your own words, although it may be to a duke or duchess, and not in those of your master or lady. For how can they understand as well as you do, who have been bred to the employment, what belongs to a message. But never deliver the answer until it is called for, and then adorn it with your own style. Likewise, you are the best judge of what acquaintance your lady ought to have. Therefore, if she sends you with a message of compliment or business to a family you do not like, deliver the answer in such a manner as may breed a quarrel between them never to be reconciled. Or, if a footman comes from the same family on a like errand, turn the answer she orders you to deliver in such a way as the other family may take it for an affront.

If your master sends you with a small trifling present

to one of his friends, be as careful of it as you would be of a diamond ring. Thus, even when the present is nothing more than half a dozen of pippin apples, send up the servant who received the message to say that you were ordered to deliver with your own hands. This will show your exactness and concern to prevent accidents or errors. In consequence, the gentleman or lady cannot do less than give you a shilling. Likewise, when your master receives a similar present, teach the messenger who brings it to do the same and also give your master hints that may stir up his generosity. For brother servants should assist one another, since it is all for your master's honour. The latter is the main concern on which every good servant should be advised, and of which he is the best judge.

When you leave your lady at church on Sundays, you have two hours safe to spend with your companions at the ale-house, or over a beefsteak and a pot of ale at home with the cook and the maids. As a matter of fact, poor servants have so few opportunities to be happy that they ought not to miss any.

Never ask leave to go out, for then it will be always known that you are absent and you will be thought an idle, rambling fellow. Whereas if you go out and nobody notices, you have a chance of coming home without being missed. You need not tell your fellow-servants where you are gone, for they will be sure to say that you were in the house but two minutes ago, which is the duty of all servants.

When you step but a few doors off to chat with a wench, or take a running pot of ale, or to see a brother footman going to be hanged, leave the street door open. In that way you may not be forced to knock and make your master discover that you have gone out. For a quarter of an hour's time can do his service no harm.

If you are sent to the post-office with a letter in a cold, rainy evening, step to the ale-house and take a pot until it is supposed you have completed your errand. But mind to take the next fair opportunity to post the letter, as becomes an honest servant.

In some households, the master often sends for a bottle of wine to the tavern and you are the messenger. Therefore, I advise you to take the smallest bottle you can find. Notwithstanding, make the publican give you a full quart, then you will get a good sup for yourself and your bottle will be filled. As for a cork to stop it, you need be at no pains, for the thumb will do as well, or a bit of dirty chewed paper.

In all disputes with chairmen and coachmen over the fare, when your master sends you down to bargain with them, take pity of the poor fellows and tell your master that they will not take a farthing less. It is more for your interest to get your share of a pot of ale, than to save a shilling to your master to whom it is but a trifle.

Never wear socks when you wait at meals; that is for your own health, as well as of those who sit at table. Most ladies like the smell of young men's toes and furthermore, it is a sovereign remedy against the vapours.

When you wait behind a chair at meals, keep constantly wriggling the back of the chair, that the person behind whom you stand may know that you are ready to attend him.

There is a great controversy about the most convenient and genteel way of holding your plate at meals. Some stick it between the frame and the back of the chair, which is an excellent expedient wherever the make of the chair will allow it. Others, fearing that the plate might fall, grasp it so firmly that their thumb reaches to the middle of the hollow. That however is no secure method, if your thumb is dry. In that case, I advise you to make sure and wet the bowl of your thumb with your tongue. As to the absurd practice of letting the back of the plate rest on the hollow of your hand, which some ladies recommend, it is universally exploded, as it is liable to so many accidents. By the way, when you carry a parcel of china plates, if they happen to fall, and it is a frequent misfortune, your excuse must be that a dog ran across you in the hall. Or that the chamber-maid accidentally pushed the door against you. That a mop stood across the entry and tripped you up. That your sleeve stuck against the key or the knob of the lock.

Other footmen are so refined that they hold their plate directly under their left armpit, which is the best way of keeping it warm. But this may be dangerous as soon as you want to take away a dish. Then your plate may happen to fall upon some of the company's heads. I myself confess to have objected against all these ways which I have often tried. Therefore, I recommend a fourth, which is to stick your plate up to the rim between your waistcoat and your shirt, in the left side. This will keep it at least as warm as under your armpit, and also hide it so that strangers may take you for a better servant, too good to hold a plate. It will also secure the plate from falling. In that position it lies ready for you to whip it out in a moment, ready warmed, to any guest within your reach who may want it. And lastly, there is another convenience in this method. If at any time during your waiting you find yourself on the point of coughing or sneezing, you can immediately snatch out your plate and hold the hollow part close to your nose or mouth. Thus you prevent spirting any droplets from either upon the dishes or the ladies' head-dress. You see, gentlemen and ladies observe a similar practice on such occasions, with the means of a hat or a handkerchief.Yet a plate is less fouled and sooner cleaned than either of the latter. For when you cough and sneeze are over, by returning your plate to the old position, your shirt will clean it in the passage.

Take off the largest dishes and set them on with one hand, to show the ladies your vigour and strength of back. But always do it between two ladies, so that if the dish happens to slip, the soup or sauce may fall on their clothes, and would not daub the floor. By this practice, two of our brethern, my worthy friends, got considerable fortunes.

When you take a dirty plate from any of the guests and notice the dirty knife and fork lying on the plate, show your dexterity: take up the plate and throw off the knife and fork on the table, without shaking off the bones or broken meat that are left. Then the guest, who has more time than you, will wipe the fork and knife already used.

When you carry dishes or other things out of the room at meals, fill both your hands as full as possible. For though you may sometimes spill and sometimes let fall, yet you will find at the year's end that you have made great dispatch, and saved abundance of time.

It is much to be lamented that gentlemen of our employment have but two hands to carry plates, dishes, bottles and the like out of the room at meals. The misfortune is all the greater because one of the hands is required to open the door, while you are encumbered with your load. In consequence, I advise you that the door may always be left ajar, to enable you to open it with your foot. Then you may carry out plates and dishes from your belly up to your chin, besides a good quantity of things under your arms, which will save you many a weary step. But take care that none of your burdens falls until you are out of the room, and if possible, out of hearing, too.

If you are ordered to break the claw of a crab or lobster, clap it between the hinges of the dining-room door. Thus you can do it gradually without mashing the meat, which often happens whenever you use they key to the front door or the pestle.

When you carry up a dish of meat, dip your fingers in the sauce or lick it with your tongue, to try and see whether it is good and fit for your master's table.

If you are bringing up a joint of meat in a dish, and were it to fall out of your hand before you get into the dining-room, take the meat gently off the ground, wipe it with the lap of your coat, put it back into the dish and serve it up. When your lady misses the sauce which you have just spilled, tell her that it is to be sent up in a plate by itself.

Whenever you carry a glass of liquor to any person who has called for it, do not bob him on the shoulder, or cry: 'Sir' or 'Madam, here's the glass.' That would be unmannerly, as if you had a mind to force it down one's throat. Rather stand at the person's right shoulder and wait his time. If he strikes it down with his elbow absent-mindedly, that is his fault and not yours.

Take care that at certain intervals during the meals, especially whenever persons of quality are present, you and your brothers be all out of the room together. In this way you will give yourselves some ease from the fatigue of waiting, and at the same time leave the company to converse more freely, unconstrained by your presence.

When you know, however, that your master is most busy in company, come in and pretend to settle about the room. If he chides you, say that you thought he had rung the bell. This will divert him from plodding on business too much, or spending himself on talk, or racking his thoughts, all which are hurtful to his constitution.

When grace is said after the meal, you and your brothers take the chairs from behind the company, so that when they go to sit again they may fall backwards, which makes them all merry.

When you take away the remaining pieces of bread after dinner, put them on the dirty plates and press them down with other plates over them, so nobody can touch them. They will go by right to the menial boy in ordinary.

When dinner is over, carry down a great heap of plates to the kitchen and when you come to the head of the stairs, trundle them all before you. There is no more agreeable sight or sound, especially if they are silver,and moreover, think of the trouble they save you. There they will lie ready near the kitchen door for the scullion to wash them.

Snuff the candles with your fingers and throw the snuff on the floor, then tread it out to prevent the stink. By this method you will very much save the snuffers from wearing out. You also ought to snuff them close to the tallow, which will make them run and so increase the perquisite of the cook's kitchen-stuff. For she is the person you ought in prudence to be well with.

In winter, light the dining-room fire but two minutes before dinner is served up, so that your master may see how sparing you are of his coals. On the other hand, when you are ordered to stir up the fire, clean away the ashes from between the bars with the fire brush.

If you are ordered to make coffee for the ladies after dinner and the pot happens to boil over, while you are running up for a spoon to stir it or are thinking of something else or struggling with the chamber-maid for a kiss, then wipe the sides of the pot clean with a dish-cloth and carry up the coffee boldly. When your lady finds it too weak and asks you whether it has not run over, deny the fact absolutely, swear you put in more coffee than ordinarily, that you never stirred an inch away from it, that you strove to make it better than usual because your mistress had ladies with her and that the other servants in the kitchen will tell her the same. Upon this, you will find that the other ladies will pronounce your coffee to be very good. Eventually your lady will confess that her mouth is out of taste. In the future she will suspect herself more and be more cautious in finding fault. This I wish you to do from a principle of conscience, for coffee is very unwholesome. Out of affection towards your lady, you ought to give it to her as weak as possible. On account of your lady's health, you may and ought to substract a third part of the powder whenever you have a mind to treat any of the maids with a dish of fresh coffee. In that way you also win her maids' good-will.

Let a shoe-boy clean your shoes first, for fear of soiling the chambers and then let him clean your master's. Keep him for that purpose and to run your errands, and for all that pay him with scraps. When you are sent on an errand, be sure to hedge in some business of your own, either to see your sweetheart or to drink a pot of ale with some brother servant, which is so much free time gained. In order to learn the secrets of other households, tell your brethern those of your master's. Thus you will grow a favourite both at home and abroad, and be regarded as a person of importance.

When you are forced to clean your master's shoes with your own hand, use the edge of the sharpest case knife and dry them with the toes an inch from the fire. Wet shoes are dangerous, and besides, in this way you will get them the sooner for yourself.

When you are in lodgings and no shoe-boy to be got, clean your master's shoes with the bottom of the curtains, a clean napkin or your landlady's apron.

When your master and lady are talking together in their bed-chamber and you have some suspicion that you or your fellow servants are concerned in what they say, listen at the door for the public good of all the servants. Likewise urge all to take proper measures in order to prevent any innovations that may hurt the community.

Be not proud in prosperity. You might have heard that Fortune turns on a wheel. If you have a good place you are at the top of the wheel. Remember how often you have been stripped and kicked out of doors, your wages all taken up beforehand and spent on reconditioned red-heeled shoes, second-hand toupees and repaired lace ruffles, besides a swinging debt to the ale-wife and the brandy-shop. The neighbouring tapster who before used to beckon you over to a savory bit of ox cheek in the morning and would give it to you gratis and only score you up for the liquor, as soon as you are packed off in disgrace will carry a petition to your master to be paid out of your wages, though you owed him nothing. Then he will pursue you with bailiffs into every blind cellar. Remember how soon you grew shabby, threadbare and out at heels. How you were forced to borrow an old livery coat to make your appearance while you were looking for a place. How you sneaked to every house where you had an old acquaintance willing to spare you a scrap to keep body and soul together. Remember how on the whole you were in the lowest station of human life, which as the old ballad goes, was that of a skipkennel turned out of a place. I say, remember all this now, in your flourishing condition. Pay your contributions to your former brothers, the younger sons, who are left to the wide world. Take one of them as your dependant, to send with your lady's messages when you have a mind to go the ale-house, instead. Privately slip him a slice of bread and a bit of cold meat now and then, your master can afford it. If he is not yet put upon the establishment for a lodging, let him lie in the stable or the coach-house or under the back stairs, and recommend him as an excellent servant to all the gentlemen who frequent your house.

Although you gentlemen in livery have the misfortune to be treated scurvily by all mankind, yet you manage to get along somehow and to keep up your spirits,and sometimes even arrive at considerable fortunes. I was an intimate friend of one of our brethern, who was a footman to a Court lady. She had an honourable employment, was sister to an earl and the widow of a man of quality. She found something so polite in my friend, the gracefulness with which he tripped before her chair and put his hair under his hat, that she made him many advances. Eventually one day taking the air in her coach with Tom behind it, the coachman mistook the way and stopped at a private chapel where the couple were married. And Tom came home in the coach by his lady's side. Unfortunately, he taught her to drink brandy, of which she died, but not before she pawned all her plate to purchase it . And Tom nowadays is a journeyman malster.

Boucher, the famous gamester, was another of our fraternity and when he was worth 50,000£, he dunned the Duke of B--m for an arrear in wages while in his service! And I could quote many other cases, and one in particular : the son of one of them came to have one of the chief offices at Court. It suffices to give you the following advice: be pert and saucy to all mankind and especially to the chaplain, the waiting-woman and the better sort of servants in the household of a person of quality. Do not mind a kicking or a caning now and then. Your insolence will at last turn to good account, and from wearing a livery, you may soon carry a pair of colours.

To grow old in the office of a footman is the highest of all indignities. Therefore, when you find years coming on, without hopes of a place at Court, a command in the Army, a succession to the stewardship, a position in the Revenue (the last two you cannot obtain without reading and writing), or running away with your master's niece or daughter, then I directly advise you to go upon the road. There, you will meet many of your old comrades and live a short and merry life and also cut a figure at your exit. Here are some instructions to that purpose.

It relates to your behaviour when you are going to be hanged either for robbing your master, house breaking, killing the first man you met or in a drunken quarrel, or for going upon the highway. That you may come to such an end is due either to love of good fellowship, a generosity of mind or too much vivacity of spirits. Your good behaviour becomes the concern of the whole community in such circumstances. At your trial deny the fact with all the solemnity of imprecations. A hundred of your brethern will attend about the bar, if they can be admitted, and be ready upon demand to give you a good character before the court. Let nothing prevail upon you to confess, but the promise of pardon for divulging your comrades. But I suppose all this to be in vain, for if you escape this time, your fate will be the same another day. Get a speech written by the best author of Newgate. Some of your kind wenches will provide you with a holland shirt and white cap crowned with a crimson or black ribbon. Take leave cheerfully of all your friends in Newgate. Mount the cart with courage; fall on your knees; lift up your eyes; hold a book in your hands although you cannot read a word; deny the fact at the gallows; kiss and forgive the hangman, and so, farewell! You shall be buried with pomp, at the charge of the fraternity. The surgeon shall not touch a limb of you, and your fame shall continue until a successor of equal fame fills your place.

THE COACHMAN

Your office binds you to nothing but to step into the box and carry your master or lady.

Let your horses be so well trained that when you attend your lady at a visit, they will wait patiently for you while you slip into a neighbouring ale-house to take a pot with a friend.

Get a menial boy to watch your coach at the church-door on Sundays, that you and your brother coachmen may be merry together at the ale-house while your master and lady are at church.

Take care that your wheels are in good repair and get a new set bought as often as you can, no matter whether you are allowed the old pair as your gratuity or not. In the former case they will turn to your honest profit. In the latter, it will be a just punishment on your master for his covetousness. And perhaps the coach-maker will consider you, too.

If you find any gentleman growing fond of one of your horses and willing to consider your trouble beside the price, then persuade your master to sell the horse. The beast has grown so vicious that you cannot undertake to drive with him any longer, and on top of it all, he is breaking down and His Honour would not be able to sell the horse anyway.

Whenever you do not feel like driving, tell your master that the horses got a cold. Or that they need shoeing. The rain is no good to them, roughens their coat and rots the harness. This piece of advice applies to the groom, too.

If your master dines with a country friend, drink as much as you can get, because it is common knowledge that a good coachman never drives so well as when he is drunk. Then show your skill by driving along a precipice, just an inch away, and keep saying that you never drive so well as when you are drunk.

THE GROOM

You are the servant upon whom the care of your master's honour during all journeys depends entirely.Your breast is its sole repository. If he travels into the country and lodges at inns, every dram of brandy, every additional pot of ale you drink, enhances his character. As a result, his reputation ought to be dear to you. And I hope, you will not be too thrifty with it either. The smith, the sadler's journeyman, the cook at the inn, the ostler and porter ought all by your means to partake of your master's generosity. Thus his fame will be spread from one county to another. What is a gallon of ale, or a pint of brandy in His Worship's pocket! And though he should belong with those who value their credit less than their purse, yet your care of the former ought to be so much greater. His horse needs two feedings. Your horse needs nails. If his allowance of oats and beans is larger than the journey requires, a third part may be retrenched and turned into ale and brandy. Thus his honour may be preserved by your discretion and less expense to him. Or if he travels with no other servant, the matter is easily settled in the bill between you and the tapster.

Therefore, as soon as you alight at the inn, deliver your horses to the stable-boy and let him gallop them to the next pond. However, when you come to your inn with the horses wet and dirty after hard riding, if they are very hot, make the ostler plunge them into water up to their bellies without delay, and allow them to drink as much as they please. But be sure to gallop them full speed a mile at least, to dry their skins and warm the water in their bellies. The ostler understands his business. Leave your master to the care of the servants in the inn and your horses to those in the stable. Thus both he and they are left in the proper hands, but you are to provide for yourself. In consequence, get your supper, drink freely and go to bed without annoying your master who is in better hands than yours. The ostler is an honest fellow, loves horses in his heart and would not wrong the dumb creatures for the world.

Be considerate of your master and order the servants not to wake him too early. Get your breakfast before he is up, that he may not wait for you. Make the ostler advise him to stay a little longer until the sky clears up, for he is afraid there will be rain and your master will have enough time after dinner.

Let your master mount before you, out of good manners. As he is leaving the inn, drop a word in favour of the ostler, what care he took of the beasts and add that you never saw more civilized servants. Let your master ride on first, while you linger on until the landlord has given you a dram. Then gallop after him through the town or village with full speed, for fear that he should want you, and also to show your horsemanship.

If you are a piece of horse-doctor, as every good groom ought to be, get sack, brandy or strong beer to rub your horses' heels every night, and be not sparing. What is left, if any is spent, you know how to dispose of. During long journeys, ask permission from your master to give ale to the horses. Carry two quarts full to the stable, pour half a pint into a bowl, and if they do not drink it, you and the ostler must do the best you can. I recommend that you never fail to repeat the experiment.

Consider your master's health and rather than let him take long journeys, say the beasts are weak and sunken with so much hard riding. Tell him of a very good inn five miles nearer than where he intended to go. Leave one of his horse's foreshoe loose in the morning. Or see to it that the saddle pinches the beast in the withers. Or keep the horse without corn all the evening before and that morning, too, so that he may tire on the road. Wedge a thin plate of iron between the hoof and the shoe to make him halt. You do all this in perfect consideration for your master's well-being.

When your master gets in his mind to ride out for the

air or for pleasure, it may happen that some private business of yours makes it inconvenient to you to attend him. On such occasions give him to understand that the horses need bleeding or purging. That his own pad has got bulges; that the saddle needs stuffing, and his bridle has been taken to be mended. This you may honestly do, because it will do no harm to the horses or to your master. At the same time it will show the great care you take of the poor dumb creatures.

When you go to air your horses in the park or in the fields, give them a horse-boy, or one of the menials, who being lighter than you, may be trusted to run races with less damage to the horses. Teach them to leap over hedges and ditches, while you are drinking a friendly pot with your brother grooms. Sometimes, however, you and they may run races yourselves for the honour of your horses and of your masters.

Never deprive your horses of hay and oats at home, but fill the rack to the top, and the manger to the brim. For you would take it ill to be deprived yourself. Although they may not have the stomach to eat, remember that they have no tongue to ask, either. If the hay falls down, there is no loss, for it will make litter and save straw.

If your master sends you to buy hay, deal with those who will be the most liberal to you. For service being no inheritance, you ought not to let slip any lawful and customary perquisite. If your master buys it himself, he wrongs you. To teach him his duty, be sure to find fault with that hay as long as it lasts. And if the horses thrive on it, the fault is yours.

Hay and oats in the hands of a skillful groom will make excellent ale as well as brandy. But this is only a hint.

When your master dines or stays at a gentleman's house in the country where there is no groom or he may be out, or where the horses have been quite neglected, be sure to employ one of the servants to hold the horse when your master mounts. You should do it yourself only when the master alights to call in for a few minutes. Otherwise, brother servants must always befriend one another. Your master's honour is at stake, because he cannot do less than give a piece of money to him who holds his horse.

When your master is leaving a gentleman's house in the country where he spent the night, then consider his honour and let him know how many servants of both sexes are in the household who expect to be tipped. At the same time, give them their cue to attend in two lines as your master leaves the house. But discourage him from trusting the money to the butler, for fear the latter might cheat the rest. This will force your master to be more generous. Then you may take the opportunity to tell your master that squire So-and-So whom you served previously always gave so much apiece to the common servants, and so much to the housekeeper and the rest. You should no less than double what he intended to give. On the other hand, be sure to tell the servants what good turn you did them. This will gain you love and to your master, honour.

If you find that the hay and oats are good at the house of the gentleman with whom your master stays, complain loud of their badness. This will get you the name of a dilligent servant. However, make sure that you cram the horses with as much oats as they can eat while you stay at that house. Then you may give them so much less for some days at the inns, and turn the rest of the oats into ale for yourself. When you leave that gentleman's house, tell your master what a greedy lump that gentleman was, that you got nothing but buttermilk or water to drink. This will make your master allow you a pot of ale the more, out of pity, at the next inn. But if you happen to get drunk in a gentleman's house, your master cannot be angry, because it costs him nothing. And so you ought to tell him that in so many words as your condition at the time permits you. Remind him that it is both for his and the gentleman's honour to make a friend's servant welcome.

If there is a particular inn in town to which you keep going and where you are well acquainted with the ostler or tapster and the people of the house, then find fault with the other inns, and recommend it to your master.

You may now and then lend your master's pad to a brother servant or to your favourite maid, for a short jaunt. Or you may hire the horse for a day, because the beast is sick for want of exercise. If your master happens to need the horse, or gets it in his mind to visit the stable, curse that rogue the helper who has gone out with the key.

When you are going to be hired and you are asked whether you are apt to be drunk, admit that you love a cup of good ale. But also that it is your way, drunk or sober, never to neglect your horses.

You may dare to be drunk much oftener than the coachman, whatever he pretends to allege on his own behalf. After all, you risk nobody's neck but your own. For the horse will probably take so much care of himself as to come off with only a strain or a shoulder slip.

A master ought always to love his groom, put him into a handsome livery and allow him a silver-laced hat. When so equipped, all the honours he receives on the road he owes them to you alone. That he is not turned out of the way by every carrier is due to the civility which he receives at second hand, from the respect paid to your livery.

When you carry your master's riding coat while on a journey, wrap your own in it, but turn your master's inside out, to preserve the outside from dampness and dirt. In this way, when it begins to rain, your master's coat will be the first to be given to him. If it gets more hurt than yours, he can afford it better, for your livery must always serve it year's apprenticeship.

If your horse drops a foreshoe, be so careful as to alight and pick it up. Then ride with all the speed you can, with the shoe in your hand so that every traveller may notice your care, to the next smith on the road. Make him put it on immediately, that your master need not wait for you, and that the poor beast may be as short a time without a shoe as possible.

When you want to spend an hour or two with your companions at the ale-house but stand in need of a reasonable excuse for your stay, leave by the back door, with an old bridle, girth or stirrup leather in your pocket. On your return, come home by the front door, with the same bridle, girth or stirrup leather dangling in your hand, as if you were coming from the saddler's where you had the same mended. If you are met by your master, you will earn the repute of a careful servant. This I know to have been practised with good success.

THE WAITING-MAID

Two incidents have happend of late to lessen the comforts and profits of your employment. One is the execrable habit, grown among ladies, of trading their old clothes for china, or of turning them into covers for easy chairs or patch-work for screens, stools, cushions and the like. The other is the invention of small chests and trunks with lock and key, in which they keep the tea and sugar. It is impossible for a waiting-maid to live without those articles. Under such circumstances, it means that you are forced to buy brown sugar and pour water upon the already brewed leaves, when they have lost all their taste and strength. I cannot think of any perfect remedy against either of these two evils. With regard to the former, I suppose that there should be a general confederacy of all the servants in every household to drive the china hawkers from the doors, for the public good. As to the latter, there is no other method to overcome it but by a false key which is a device both difficult and dangerous to acquire. As concerns the honesty in procuring one I am in no doubt, particularly when your lady gives you so just a provocation by denying you an ancient and lawful privilege. The mistress of the tea-shop may now and then give you half an ounce, but that will be only a drop in the bucket. As a result, I am afraid you will be forced to run in trust and like the rest of your sisters, pay for it out of your own wages as far as they will go. You can easily supplement your wages in other ways, if your lady is handsome or her daughters have good fortunes.

If you are with a great family, as My Lady's woman, My Lord may probably like you, though you are not half so handsome as his own lady. In that case, take care to get as much out of him as you can. Never allow him the smallest liberty nor even the squeezing of your hand, unless he puts a guinea into it. So, by degrees, make him pay accordingly for every new attempt, doubling upon him in proportion to the concessions you allow and always struggling and threatening to cry out or tell your lady, although you receive his money. Five guineas for handling your breast is a cheap pennyworth, though you seem to resist with all your might. But never allow him the last favour under a hundred guineas, or a settlement of twenty pounds a year for life.

In such a household, if you are handsome, you will have the choice of three lovers: the chaplain, the steward and My Lord's gentleman. I would advise you to choose the steward. But if you happen to be young with child by My Lord, you must take up with the chaplain. I like My Lord's gentleman the least of the three. He is usually vain and insolent as soon as he is off duty and sheds his livery. Besides, if he misses the occasion to enlist in the Army a couple of times, or if he fails to get a place as a customs clerk, his only remedy is the highway.

I must warn you particularly against My Lord's eldest son. If you are smart enough, the odds are that you may induce him to marry you and make you a lady. On the other hand, if he is a common rake, which most of the times he is, avoid him like satan, for he stands in less awe of a mother, than My Lord does of a wife. And after ten thousand promises, you will get nothing from him but clap or a big belly, and more likely, both together.

If you are so lucky as to wait on a young lady with a great fortune, you must be a very bad manager if you cannot get five or six hundred pounds for yourself by disposing of her. Do not tire of putting in her mind that she is rich enough to make any man happy. That there is no real happiness but in love. That she has the freedom to choose wherever she pleases and not under the compulsion of her parents who never make allowances for innocent passion. That there is a world of handsome, fine, sweet and young gentlemen in town, who would be glad to die at her feet. That the conversation of two lovers is heaven upon earth. Tell her that love, like death, equals all conditions. Which means that if she should cast her eyes upon a young fellow below her in birth and estate, his marrying her would make him a gentleman. That yesterday, on the Mall, you saw the prettiest ensign, who to you was as good as forty thousand pounds. On the other hand, take care that everybody knows what lady you are waiting on, how great a favourite of hers you are, and that she always takes your advice. Go often to St James's Park, because there the fine fellows will soon discover you and will try to slip a letter into your sleeve or your bosom. Pull it out in a fury and throw it on the ground, unless you find at least two guineas along with it. In the latter case, seem not to find it and to think that he was playing only the practical joker with you. As soon as you are back home, drop the letter carelessly in your lady's chamber.There she finds it and is angry. Protest that you knew nothing of it. The only thing you could remember was that a gentleman in the park attempted to kiss you, and you believe that it was he who put the letter in your sleeve or petty-coat unawares. Indeed, he was a pretty a man as she ever saw. That she may burn the letter if she pleases. As a matter of course, if your lady is wise, she will burn some other piece of paper in your presence and keep the letter and read it when you are gone downstairs. You must follow this practice as often as you safely can. But let him who happens to pay you best with every letter be also the handsomest man.

If a footman allegedly brings a letter to the house to be delivered by you to your lady, throw it at his head, even if it comes from your best customer. Call the messenger impudent rogue and villain and shut the door in his face. As a proof of fidelity, run up to your lady and tell her what you have done.

If you serve a lady who is little disposed to gallantries, you will find wise to pay attention to three things in particular. Firstly, how to please your lady. Secondly, how to prevent suspicion in the husband, and lastly, but not in the least, how to make the most out of it for your own benefit. To give you full directions in this important matter would require a large volume. All rendez-vous at home are dangerous both to your lady and yourself. Therefore do your best to have them in a third place. That is especially necessary when your lady entertains more than one lover, which is a hundred odds as it is. Each of them is more jealous than a thousand husbands. However, very unlucky coincidences may often happen even under the best management. I need not warn you of employing your good offices mainly in favour of those whom you find the most liberal. Nonetheless, if your lady should happen to cast an eye upon a handsome footman, you should be generous enough to bear with her whim which is no oddity but a very natural appetite. It is still the safest of all the home intrigues. Formerly it was also the least suspected, but no longer, as it has grown more common. In such situations, the greatest danger is that when dealing with that kind of gentry, too often it may happen that you are dealing in bad ware. Then, indeed, your lady and you are in a very bad way, though not altogether desperate.

But to say the truth, I confess that it is a great presumption in me to offer you any instructions in the conduct of your lady's affairs. Your whole sisterhood is so expert already and so deeply learned in such matters. They are so much more difficult to outline than the assistance which my brother footmen extend to their masters on the like occasions. Therefore, I leave it to be treated by some abler pen.

When a footman comes with a polite message to inquire how your lady does when she is ill and getting a little nap in the morning after a very bad night, do not let the compliment be lost. Shake her gently until she wakes up. Then deliver the message, receive her answer and let her go back to sleep.

If you lock up a silk mantua or a laced bonnet in a trunk or chest, leave a piece out, so you may know where to find it when you open the trunk again.

THE CHAMBER-MAID

The nature of your employment differs according to the quality, the pride or the wealth of the lady you serve. On the other hand, as this treatise is to be applied to all sorts of families, I find myself in great difficulty to define the business for which you are hired. In a family that enjoys a tolerable estate, your office differs from that of the house-maid. Then your particular province is your lady's chamber, where you make the bed and keep things in order. If you live in the country, you also take care of the rooms of the lady guests, which brings all the tips that fall to your share. Your usual lover, as I take it, is the coachman. But if you are under twenty and tolerably handsome, perhaps a footman may cast his eyes on you.

Get your favourite footman to help you in making your lady's bed. If you serve a young couple, the footman and you will make the prettiest observations in the world while you are turning up the bed-cloths. When whispered about, they will be very entertaining to the whole household and will get among the neighbourhood, too

Making beds in hot weather is very laborious work and you will be apt to sweat. Therefore, when you find the drops running down from your forehead, wipe them off with a corner of the sheet that may not be seen on the bed. When you put a clean pillow-case on your lady's pillow, fasten it well with three corking pins to make sure that it will not fall off during the night.

When you bar the window-shutters of your lady's bed-chamber at night, leave open the sashes, to let in the fresh air and sweeten the room. While you leave the windows open for air in daytime, leave books or something else on the window-seat that they may get air, too.

When you are ordered to open or lock any door, trunk, or cabinet and miss the proper key, or cannot distinguish it from the bunch, try the first key that you can thrust in and turn it with all your strength. Exert yourself until you open the lock or break the key. Otherwise, your lady will reckon you a fool to come back and do nothing.

When you spread bread and butter for tea, be sure that all the holes in the loaf be left full of butter to keep the bread moist for dinner. Likewise, let the mark of your thumb be seen upon one end of every slice, to show your cleanliness.

When your lady sends you to wash a china cup and it happens to fall, bring it up and swear that you did but touch it with your hand when it broke into three halves. And there I must inform you as well as your fellow-servants that you ought never to be without an excuse. It does no harm to your master and it lessens your fault. Take this instance. I do not commend you for breaking the cup. It is certain you did not break it on purpose and it is quite possible that the cup broke in your hand.

When you are tiding your lady's room, never stay to pick up dirty smocks, handkerchiefs, pinners, pin-cushions, tea-spoons, ribbons, slippers or whatever lies in your way. But sweep all in a corner and then you may take them up in a lump and save time.

Wear your lady's smock when she has thrown it off. It will do you credit, save your own linen and be not a pin in the worse.

Sometimes you want so much to watch a funeral, a quarrel, a man going to be hanged, a wedding, a procuress carted or the like. As they pass by in the street, you lift the sash suddenly and there, by ill luck it sticks. This is no fault of yours. Young women are curious by nature. You have no remedy but to cut the cord. Lay the blame upon the carpenter, if nobody saw you, and then you are as innocent as any servant in the house.

As I have already said, at times in some households you may be employed in the cleaning of your lady's rooms. Then if you happen to break any china with the top of the wisk on the mantelpiece or the cabinet, gather up the fragments, put them together as well as you can and place them behind the rest. When your lady discovers them, you may safely say that they had been broken long ago, before your time in her service. This will save your lady many an hour's vexation.

Sometimes it happens that a looking-glass is broken by the same means. While you are looking another way as you sweep the chamber, the long end of the brush strikes against the glass and breaks it to shivers. This is the worst of all misfortunes, because it is impossible to conceal. Such a fatal accident once happened in a great household where I had the honour to be a footman. I will relate the particulars to show the ingenuity of the poor chamber-maid on so sudden and dreadful an emergency. Perhaps it may help to sharpen your power of invention, if your evil star should ever give you the like occasion. The poor girl had broken a large Japan glass of great value with a stroke of her brush. She had not been contemplating the situation long when by a prodigious presence of mind she locked the door, stole into the yard, brought a stone of three pounds' weight into the chamber and laid it on the hearth, just under the looking-glass. Then she broke a pane in the sash-window that looked in the same yard. As soon as that was done, she closed the door and went about her other tasks. Two hours later, the lady went into the room, saw the glass broken, the stone lying under it and a whole pane in the window shattered. From the circumstances, she concluded just what the maid had wanted her to, that some idle straggler in the neighbourhood, or perhaps one of the out-servants had through malice, accident or carelessness flung in the stone and done the mischief. Thus far everything went well and the girl concluded that she was out of danger. But it was her bad luck that a few hours later in came the parson. The lady, naturally, told him about the mishap which you may believe had much upset her. But the minister happened to understand mathematics. He examined the situation of the yard, the window and the chimney and soon convinced the lady that the stone could have never reached the looking-glass without first taking three turns in its flight from the hand that threw it. The maid was strictly examined as soon as it was found out that she had swept the room, the same morning. However she swore upon her salvation and offered to take her oath on the Bible before his Reverence, maintaining she was as innocent as the child unborn. Yet, the poor wench was turned off. I take it to have been hard treatment, considering her ingenuity. None-theless, this may be a lesson to you, to contrive a story that will better hang together. For instance, you may say that while you were at work with the mop or the brush, a flash of lightning came suddenly at the window, which almost blinded you. That you immediately heard the ringing of broken glass on the hearth. That as soon as you recovered your sight, you saw the looking-glass all broken to pieces. Or you may allege that seeing the glass a little covered with dust, you set very gently to wipe it. Yet apparently the moisture of the air had dissolved the glue or the cement and as a result it fell to the ground. Or, as soon as the mischief is done, you may cut the cords that fastened the glass to the wainscot and let it fall flat on the floor. Run out in fright, tell your lady, curse the upholsterer and confess how narrowly you escaped from it falling upon your head. I offer such expedients from a desire I have to defend the innocent. For innocent you certainly must be if you did not break the glass on purpose. The latter alternative I would by no means excuse, except upon great provocation.

Oil the tongs, poker and fire-shovel, handle and all, not only to keep them from rusting, but likewise to prevent meddling people from wasting your master's coals by stirring the fire.

When you are in haste, sweep the dust into a corner of the room, but leave the brush upon it so it may not be seen, for that would disgrace you.

Never wash your hands or put on a clean apron until you have made your lady's bed, for fear of rumpling your apron or dirtying your hands again.

THE HOUSE-MAID

If your master and lady go into the country for a week or more, never wash the bed-chamber or the dining-room until an hour before they are due back. Thus the rooms will be perfectly clean to receive them and you will be spared the trouble to wash them again before long.

When you wash any of the rooms towards the street late in the day, throw the dirty water out of the front door into the street, but make sure that you do not look before you do that, for fear that those on whom the water lights might think you uncivil, and that you did it on purpose. If the unfortunate passer-by breaks the windows in revenge and your lady scolds you and gives you firm orders that you should carry the pail down and empty it into the sink, you have an easy remedy. As soon as you happen to wash the floor of an upper room, carry down the pail, letting the water dribble on the stairs all the way down to the kitchen. In this way not only your burden will be lighter, but you will also convince your lady that it is better to throw the water out of the windows or down the steps of the front door. Besides, this latter practice will be very diverting to you and the whole household on a frosty evening to watch a hundred people fall on their noses or backsides before your door, when the water is frozen.

Brush down the cobwebs with a broom that is wet and dirty, which will make them stick faster to it and bring them down more efficiently.

If your lady is so nice that she will have the room scoured with freestone, be sure to leave the marks of the freestone six inches deep round the bottom of the wainscot. In this way your lady will see that you heeded her orders.

When you clean up the parlour hearth in the morning, throw the last night's ashes into a sieve. What falls through as you carry it down will serve as sand for the room and the stairs.

Bring none but large coals to the dining-room and to your lady's chamber. They make the best fires. And if you find them too big, it is easy to break them on the marble hearth.

You may consider polishing and brightening the marble hearths and the chimney-pieces with a cloth that has been dipped in grease. Nothing makes them shine so well. After all it is the business of the ladies to take care of their pettycoats.

When you have scoured all the brasses and irons in the parlour chimney, lay the dirty, wet cloth upon the next chair, so your lady may see that you have not neglected your work. Observe the same rule when you clean the brass locks. Only do not forget to leave the marks of your fingers on the doors to show your industry.

Leave the pail with the mop in it, the coal-box, a broom, a bottle, a chamber-pot and such other unsightly things either in a blind entry or upon the darkest part of the stairs that they may not ben seen. If people break their shins by trampling on them, it is their own fault.

Never empty the chamber-pots until they are quite full. At night, empty them into the street. In the morning, into the garden. It would be an endless chore to go down a dozen of times from the garret and upper rooms down to the back sides. Never wash them but in their own liquid: what proper girl would be dabbling in other folks' urine! Moreover, as I observed before, the smell is excellent in covering the vapours. Or you may consider leaving your lady's jordan in the bed-chamber window all day to air.

When your lady's bed is made you may put the chamber-pot under it and thrust the valance along with the pan. In that way it will remain in full sight and ready for your lady when she has occasion to use it.

I am very much offended with those ladies who are so proud and lazy that they would readily step into the garden to pluck a rose, but keep that odious implement in the bed-chamber itself, or at least in the dark closet adjoining the chamber, in order to ease their worst necessities in it. Usually you are expected to carry the pan out, which makes not only the chamber but also your clothes offensive to all who come near. Now, in order to cure them of this odious practice, let me advise you. You should carry it down the great stairs openly and in the presence of the footmen. If anybody knocks at the street door while you have the filled vessel in your hands, make them open it. If anything can, this will make your lady take pains of evacuating her person in the proper place, rather than expose her filthiness to all the callers and the male servants in the house.

Lock up a cat or a dog in some room or closet, so that the noise they would kick all over the house may frighten the thieves, if any would attempt to break or steal in.

When you go to bed, make sure to put out the fire and so blow out the candle with your breath and then thrust it under your bed. For the smell of snuff is very good against vapours.

Persuade the footman who got you with child to marry you before you are six months gone. If your lady asks you why you would take that fellow who is not worth fourpence, let your answer be that service is no inheritance.

FINIS

A COMMENTARY

by Simona Draghici

CORRIGENDUM

On page 73, line 20, read 'are' instead of 'is', and line 24, read 'demands' instead of 'does not demand'.

A COMMENTARY

Apparently a diffuse prejudice has prevented this work by Jonathan Swift to gain the popularity which it deserves. Whoever reads it properly soon becomes aware that it is as much a book about the stupidity of domestic servants as, say, Part IV of GULLIVER'S TRAVELS is about the wisdom of horses. After all, Swift includes in his category of servants everybody who, for one reason or another, trades his or her own services in exchange of a fee payable in cash or in kind. Servants, in his opinion, are all those who expect to derive a direct, material reward from those who engage their efforts to meet one particular need or another, whether sanctioned by convention or not. Their behaviour is inherently logical within these terms, or one should say economical. Servants are likely to minimize the expenditure of their efforts and maximize returns as long as they rely on their abilities as their means of physical survival, source of income and capital: '...a servant is not to be blamed if he strives to better himself. Tell them that service is no inheritance, that your work is more than what it ought to be and your wages are very small'(p.15). It is in the light of this that a passion for gambling in the employer may prove a lucrative opportunity for the servant catering for it: 'If your lady loves to play cards, your fortune is made for ever. Moderate gambling will bring you ten shillings a week in revenue... It is all ready cash and got without labour'(p.25).

Rather, we are holding in our hands a book on individualism avant la lettre, so to speak, that is before it became an ideology and an ethical value with either positive or negative connotations. Swift points to the individualism generated and perpetuated by intensive and prolonged physical and social mobility that accompany political revolutions. The individualism outlined by Swift in this book is that state of things social that engenders a sense of self-reli-

ance as one's only means of survival in the absence of any outside, objective structure that would designate one's position within the social network, regulate one's relations with the others and which, in short, would make provisions for one's preservation and reproduction.

Neither is the fun which exhudes from almost every page derivative from the cudgelling of simpletons. It is by far more complex. Actually, besides the humour generated by the misuse of words, as in the case of the cup that 'broke in three halves'(p.60), that is to say, the quite superficial laughter caused by the use of puns, we come across two major sources. They are as profound as they are universal. One is the irony of consequences, and the other is the pseudologic resorted to in one's attempts to overcome the crisis unleashed by one or more of the unintended consequences of one's acts.

In this book, the irony of consequences surges mostly from the application of a certain pattern of conduct or action to situations that according to social conventions require a different pattern. Implicitly it also shows the actor's failure to envision, and so avoid, as many of the possible secondary effects of his intended action. Thus expediency pursued with single-mindedness is likely to disregard what could happen to the instruments used in the process (p.14). However, in order to enjoy the dead-pan humour fully, the reader must get into the actor's shoes and envisage for him- or herself the consequences which might result in practice from the applications and illustrations set forth in Swift's treatise. Otherwise, 'if one does not understand horses,' one cannot appreciate the humour which Swift invests in his description of the treatment applied to a hard-driven pair by the ostler at the inn, for instance. Swift invites his readers' participation in the cathartic mirth in which he sees a solution albeit temporary yet accessible to any mortal who is endlessly and helplessly confronted by the infinite number of complexities inherent in human social existence, the more unpredictable as the social grid grows looser.

The other main source of humour is related to it, as

it refers to those attempts, verbal or otherwise, that are made to patch up, so to speak, the situation torn to pieces by the unintended consequences of one's acts. The urgency of such a task, which in the implicit transition from one qualitative state to another demands speed and the previously wanting acumen, finds in pseudologic the only readily available empirical instrument to use in order to restore the state of equilibrium: 'If your dinner fails in almost every dish, how could you help it! You were teased by the footmen coming into the kitchen. And to prove it true, take the occasion to be angry and throw a ladleful of broth on one or two of their liveries. Moreover, Friday and Childermas-day are two cross days in the week, and that is impossible to have good luck on either of them. Therefore, on those days you have a lawful excuse'(p.33). Indeed, Swift's humour lies here in the incongruity of the justifications, and here, too, one needs to be familiar with quite a range of particular patterns of behaviour prescribed by specific social conventions for particular circumstances, and which in more settled social entities are gathered under the general name of common sense. In conditions of high and prolonged physical and social mobility, common sense is defficient, and simpler patterns of conduct, more in the line of improvisation, and in keeping with the economics of service as outlined above, are likely to be favoured instead.

The individualism of service for material gain in the absence of inheritance and in the conditions of intensive physical and social mobility is innocent of the ethics of individual responsibility: 'When you have done something wrong, be always pert and insolent, and behave as if you were the injured person. This will immediately put your master or lady off their mettle'(p.7). Two centuries later, Bertold Brecht came to a similar conclusion in a period of political turmoil when he wrote that Zuerst ist das Fressen und dann kommt die Moral. *Instead, one witnesses the generalized practice of the scapegoat. The latter is used to restore the precarious balance disturbed by the unintended consequences of one's action(s): 'When a servant is turned off, all his faults must be revealed, although most of them were never known by your master or lady. All the mischiefs done by the others should be charged to him. And if they ask why you never brought any of them to their attention, the answer should be: Sir (or Madam), really I was afraid it would make you angry. And besides, you might have thought it was malice in me'(p.9).Thus implicitly, Swift relates individual social responsibility to the condition of that kind of social structure that allows inheritance to develop and concomitantly breed a sense of personal responsibility with its intrinsic concern for the well-being of the others and a readiness to commit oneself entirely to its redress when the consequences of one's acts endanger that well-being. However, unlike a great many of the liberals of the following century, keen on emulating what they saw as the manorial ethos, Swift leaves no doubt that he considers inheritance, as unearned wealth, in itself no guarantee of socially responsible conduct. Particularly whenever it is come upon suddenly, and the recipient is unprepared to see in it anything but a collection of material assets the purpose of which is exclusively to indulge one's whims.*

Intensive and prolonged social and physical mobility also render socialization problematic: as the old customs and mores become questionable, new conventions and prescriptions are given little chance to take root. Hence superficial approximations of what faulty memories recall of past forms of conduct and etiquette are extended to situations perceived as similar to a degree. Appearances become the main, if not the sole, criterion of social differentiation: 'If you can, choose the service where your livery colours are least tawdry and eye-catching. ...That together with your master's linen, and a natural and improved confidence will give you the title you please, in whatever place you are not known'(p.35). In such a loose social context, material proof of a performed action also tends to become more important than its result in the valuation of any service rendered. Whenever standards of achievement are shaky, the qualitative appreciation of results is questionable, too. To this shift of focus the economic conduct with its effort-saving contributes substantially and in turn is favoured by it. That the plate has been polished is not to be assessed by its brightness, but by the amount of polishing powder that is left in the chinks of the plate. Thus servants are likely to take advantage of the uncertainty of standards, of wavering tastes and needs, and outbid their employers in the bluff, for the economic reasons mentioned earlier.

In such circumstances, wits and ingenuity make up for the lack of formal training which is also held in low esteem like everything that is not easily attainable (or effort-consuming), or which brings no apparent, short-term profit. Books are used to singe fowl for the table and hygiene is a luxury.

The absence of an ethics of personal responsibility from the social context of relations grounded in remunerated service also reflects upon the way the agents in interaction regard one another; their attitude towards each other is likely to be utilitarian in the sense that the others are of concern only in terms of their instrumental value. Personal relations, beyond merely accidental conviviality, is narrowed down to barter, whenever hard currency is not made to circulate. As soon as one of the parties loses its exchange potential, it is dumped unceremoniously, unless the craving for revenge or redress does not demand an even harsher treatment. The importance which appearances assume, grafted on the exchange value of individual instrumentality and in the conditions of high mobility, engenders another craving, that for fame which is intrinsically ephemeral. However, the latter is looked up to as an apotheosis, a state to be attained at the conclusion of one's life. In that way, one is freed from any possible obligation that fame may entail and at the same time is given the chance to taste the illusion of immortality. Actually short-lived, fame is cultivated by the infamous who in this way can indulge themselves, bask in the fame which they bestow on one of them for a brief moment, on his or her way out and at very little cost for themselves. The cathartic performance is worth the money, so to speak, for it justifies and reassures oneself in one's eyes and in those of the others.

On the other hand, the individualism outlined by Swift tends to be its own judge and law court in one, in the absence of a more formal and efficient system of justice. Individual retaliation for grievances becomes conventional and any perceived injustice frees the victim from any moral constraint in his or her attempts to find satisfaction. The individualism of physical and social mobility also unravels the often unsuspected yet inherent political power of each human being in part, irrespective of the position occupied in the network of social relationships. Swift points to its subversive aspect by drawing his characters as capable of overturning any decision perceived as detrimental to their personal interests. It is subtle and intricate in the forms it assumes, because it is meant to remain undetected. Remember the story of the footman forced to carry his master's lantern in the street. The looser the social network, the higher the mobility, the more arbitrary the demands, the higher the risks and the chances of failure through the resistance opposed by the others. The late Stanford Professor Richard T. LaPierre talked about it in his SOCIAL PSYCHOLOGY two hundred years later. There, where material wealth is concerned, the chances of its transfer and of its destruction are as high. Sir Walter Scott came to find that out at his own expense, which also made him appreciate Swift's DIRECTIONS TO SERVANTS above many other books.

As a form of interaction, barter may be regarded at least socially as superior to the so-called natural law of the jungle, or rather in this case, of the highway, where each man is potentially a wolf onto the other. Nonetheless, its exclusive and indiscriminate application is likely to render it as disruptive socially and politically through its undesired consequences. 'The Iranian Affair,' which exploded in Washington DC late in 1986, gave one a taste of that effect.

The fact that remunerated service, though economic and so logical, may be wealth-destructive whenever used in the place of other, situationally more adequate, forms of social intercourse, brings us by the back door, so to speak, to Swift's concept of politics. The way in which he presents it is one of the most entertaining, one must admit. Interests differ and the means used to avoid their coming into collision, or if they have already collided, to handle the consequent crisis, with the restoration of normality in view, belong to the political sector. In Swift's opinión, the concern of politics is to deflate crises and assure those conditions that favour what is perceived as normal social intercourse. They, politics, proceed by redefining social situations in ways that would be found acceptable by all the parties involved. Remember the incident of the boiled-over coffee pot (p.42). The crisis is caused by the mistress bringing into the open her conflict with the footman about the brew served by him. The altercation may be more annoying to some of the guests present than the actual taste of the coffee itself. Generalized, the crisis is deflated when some take the initiative and redefine the situation by declaring the quality of the coffee in question excèllent. Concerned for the welfare of her guests, the mistress takes the cue, redefines her own stand and indirectly assumes responsibility for her own outburst which had unleashed the crisis in the first place. Indeed, none of the actors involved in that incident shows any political genius, and besides, there are other ways of preventing and diffusing such crises. Nevertheless, all that does not alter the nature of their interaction, which is political. Politics, Swift points out, are more pervasive than one would suspect. Although they bring about wars and revolutions, they are also irreplaceable in the deflation of conflictual situations. The less stable a social entity, the greater its use of politics to maintain and reproduce itself. (Whenever stability is perceived generally as the main feature of a particular social entity, there politics yield to social administration and distributive justice.) Yet, as the lady displeased with her coffee shows, politics imply not only involvement, that is concern for the others' well-being, but also the assumption of social responsibility for it, with all the negative consequences the act may have for oneself.

One may still ask why Swift had chosen domestic servants to personify his ideas and to compile his treatise on individualistic conduct in a highly mobile world. The reasons are several, and here I shall offer a couple only, to set at ease the minds of philistines; whether I would succeed is another matter. Like many of his articulate friends, and as the events evolved, Swift found himself increasingly under the close supervision of official censors anxious to discourage the slightest gesture of dissention. Besides, the Whigs could never forgive him for turning his coat. As he grew older he also became less inclined to play with the fire. Although himself never imprisoned, his publishers had been running great risks by printing his writings. One of them was even sentenced to capital punishment and executed. On the other hand, domestic servants, though in great number in the days before the industrial revolution, were less likely to sue him for libel because they lacked organization, in the modern sense *of the word. Furthermore, housekeeping, which lent itself to hyperbole and* so *enabled Swift to make his points more graphic,* proves *to be a convenient medium for his kind of humour: logical, economic conduct is quite difficult to apply to it. After all housekeeping in the main involves consumption and sanitation. Moreover, it was a medium that offered him an opportunity to record some of the foibles which crush-courses in socialization tend to breed in any exceptionally mobile society, while remaining on grounds familiar to his potential readers without incurring the risks of connivance in sedition.*

To the modern reader I would also like to suggest another allegorical reading of the book, in which the master and his lady may be seen as embodying the commonweal or the res publica, *if you wish, on the one hand, and the servants, all those who make a living or derive additional benefits at its expense, on the other. Consider the following paragraph, for instance, in this light: 'The cook, the butler, the groom, the market-man and every other servant who is involved in the household expenses, should act as if his master's whole estate ought to be applied to that servant's particular business. Thus, for instance, if the cook computes the master's estate to amount to a thousand pounds a year, he or she would reasonably conclude that a thousand pounds a year will afford enough meat, and so need not be saving. The butler in turn makes the same judgment, and so may the groom and the coachman. Every branch of expense will be filled to your master's honour' (p.9). One may come to think of the national budget deficit....*

Swift is a moral writer and he never fails to convey a message. The one that seems to me most significant nowadays in connection with this piece of writing of his, is that about the need of bringing and keeping in equilibrium public interests and the interests of the individual, which is the more difficult to achieve the larger and the more mobile the polity. If we ignore the individual, he will take his revenge by subverting the commonweal even if eventually he is to pay for it with his life. On the other hand, if we ignore the commonweal, the individual is likely to disintegrate, too, for the lack of social terms of reference. The cook ceases to be a cook as soon as his or her skills find no outlet, as the master's credit and also his capital are exhausted. However impeccably moral the justifications of one's acts, little if anything can then be done to save the master, let alone his honour.

SIMONA DRAGHICI

About the Editor

SIMONA DRAGHICI is an European-American social scientist who among other things holds a PhD degree in sociology from the University of Texas at Austin. Her interests in the comparative study of social institutions have led her more recently to the analysis of the recurrent phenomenon of civilizational decline.